I0503423

Table of Contents

Preface

You are sitting in your cubicle late one Friday afternoon. You just completed a status report on a very important project when you get a call from your boss. He congratulates you on your progress and expresses his appreciation for your ability to adjust to the complexities of changing technology. You smile and thank him as you prepare to return to your office and get ready for a weekend of skiing with your friends.

As you head for the door, he asks you to be the Master of Ceremony for an upcoming conference. Many high level executives will be there and he has bragged about your talents and abilities. He explains that you will be tasked to introduce several of the speakers, give them a tour of the plant and a brief overview of the mission of your company. You confidently thank him as you walk out the door, sweat now pouring from your forehead.

You understand technology but are petrified by the thought of having to speak to such an important group of people. Other than the speech class you took in high school, you have never spoken to a crowd of people except in your fraternity house in college. That speech was not exactly the kind your boss would want you to give.

You return to your cubicle, sweating even harder, and start googling speeches, introductions, speaker comments and anything that could help you. You remember those business self-help books at the copy shop. Then you come across *Business Recitations: Words that Welcome, Show Appreciation, and Inspire.* You page through the chapters…

Problem solved…you'll be president of the company before you know it!

1-Speaker Introductions

Today, we are honored to have (speaker's name) with us. His/her credentials include (list credentials) and past jobs include (list jobs held). Please join me in welcoming (Person's name).

*****

Our profession is replete with many challenges leading to great rewards. The rewards are the fruit of smart work and determination. Our speaker for today epitomizes the best of our vocation.

His/her education includes (list credentials) and he/she has worked at (list jobs held and current job). A respected leader in our business, please join me in welcoming (person's name).

*****

We are honored to have (person's name and company) with us today. He/she will speak to us about (topic). Let us all greet (person's name).

*****

We are delighted to have with us (person's name) of (name of business). He/She will discuss (topic) and offer recommendations as to how we can help each other in achieving our mutual goals. We welcome (person's name).

*****

Our profession is related to many other professions. Today, we are honored to have (person's name) from (name of company) who will give us insight as to how we can work together in the pursuit of networking success.

*****

Business is a team activity which requires interaction with other professions. Our speaker today is imminently qualified to speak to us about (name topic). He/She served as (work history) and is now (list present job). Please join me in welcoming (name person).

*****

Today our speaker is (name) He/She is presently working as (job title) and has served in the past as (past jobs). We are delighted he/she could join us today. Please join in a hearty welcome to (person's name).

*****

Our speaker today has done much to promote commerce on several fronts. He/She served as (list various jobs) and now is (list present position). Please, let us welcome (person's name).

$$*****$$

It is very seldom that we have the opportunity to hear such a distinguished speaker. Our speaker's life is a testimony to hard work, determination and technical expertise in his/her field. He/She was educated at (list schools) and presently serves as (present job). Let us welcome (person's name).

$$*****$$

It is always a pleasure to hear from someone who has "been there and done that." Our speaker today fits that role. He/She has worked as (list prior jobs) but most importantly, he/she has a desire to help others learn from his/her experience. With no further delay, please let's welcome (person's name)

$$*****$$

Someone once said "experience is the best teacher." However, I have learned that some experiences should be avoided. I will take someone else's word on the ones to avoid. Today, we have the opportunity to learn from someone else's experiences. Our speaker went to school at (list school) and has worked as (list past jobs). Presently, he/she serves as (list present job). Ladies and gentlemen, please welcome (speaker's name).

*****

Today's speaker is a leader in the business of (list area). He/She also is a mentor to those in our business--new and old. His/her work experience includes (positions held). We are indeed honored to be audience to such a distinguished guest. Please join me in welcoming (person's name).

*****

2-Replies to Introductions

Thank you for such an introduction. I hope my words befit such a preamble.

*****

With such an introduction one feels humbled; now please allow me to get into my address before pride sets in.

*****

Thank you for such kind words. May all of your speakers be as honored as I am by you and this great organization.

*****

Thank you. I only wish that my boss could have heard those words, although he/she might have been confused as to whom you were introducing.

*****

Thank you very much. Your kind words shall long be remembered.

*****

Such words of introduction and praise are replete with verbal calories. I hope my speech warrants them.

*****

It is a pleasure for me to address such an august crowd even if it isn't August. I hope my words will encourage, motivate and stimulate each of you to higher accomplishments.

*****

If the introducer speaks as well as he/she introduces, I would rather hear him/her speak. Those wonderful words challenge me to share truths that will help make a difference in your lives.

*****

May the message that follows such a wonderful introduction empower you to be better professionals. Thank you for your kind words.

*****

Thank you for such a nice introduction. I only hope I can deliver what you promised.

*****

To be the recipient of such an introduction warms my heart. May the words that follow do the same for yours.

*****

That was a great introduction! Let's give (introducer's name) an applause for such a great job. Now I hope that I can earn what was said.

*****

No single person could earn such an introduction. I want to begin by thanking everyone who helped me along the way. They are an integral part of the team I represent. So I shall tell them of your applause.

*****

No one person should be so bold as to accept such a wonderful introduction. Each of us in the business community must give thanks, at a time like this, to the unseen people who helped us succeed. They are the ones to who should receive your applause.

*****

The best reply to such an introduction is a message that moves each listener from the position of hearer to that of a doer. Let's give it a try.

*****

Such a gracious introduction is greatly appreciated; however, I cannot take full credit for such accomplishments. Your kind words and applause go to a large number of people working behind the scenes to make this day possible. May my brief comments bring honor to their efforts.

*****

I am temped to take credit for such an introduction; however, that would not be right. I represent the tip of an iceberg that is anchored by a fine supporting cast, and to them I direct your kind words and applause.

*****

3-After Speech Comments

We have all been challenged to raise our level of competence to a higher level. May the words we've heard today stay in our memories as we move about our daily responsibilities. Thank you, (speaker's name), for sharing with us.

*****

After hearing such an address, one cannot remain the same. This was a call to excellence. Each of us can improve our production and the place and time to start is here and now. As we leave here, lets resolve to put into practice the things we learned here today.

*****

If this speech did not move you, your anchor is stuck. Each of us was called to a higher level of greatness by our speaker. Let's go forth and do what it takes to better serve our customers.

*****

Well, we heard the call to battle. Each of us must give our reply, which will be evidenced by our actions after we leave here today. Thank you, (speaker's name), for a clear call to excellence.

*****

What shall our answer be to such a speech? If we remain the same, we lose. If we avail ourselves to the wisdom we heard, we'll be a greater help to our company and our customers. The decision is ours--please make the right choice.

*****

The best way to show our appreciation for such motivational words is to apply what we learned. Thank you, (speaker's name), for your address.

*****

I cannot fully express my appreciation for such fine words. Suffice it to say that we should each strive to apply the principles espoused by our speaker. Thank you, (speaker's name), for your motivational words.

*****

After listening to such a speech, each of us is richer. Let's not squander the wealth we gained, but apply it to help our customers and thereby our companies.

*****

If we heed the information we have just heard, there will be no limit to our production. I believe the best way to show our appreciation is to put it into practice. Let's do it rather than just talk about it.

*****

Someone once said, "imitation is the best form of flattery." We can flatter our speaker by imitating the principles he spoke about today. Indeed, his/her words deserve our consideration and application. Thank you, (speaker's name), for those seeds of future fruit.

*****

Need I say more? Such wisdom comes with its own commentary and our challenge is to go forth and to apply this message. If we do it with diligence and urgency, our customers and our company will be dual winners in the arena of commerce.

*****

The words we just heard will move us to greater success only if applied. Like a game winning play, these strategies will produce champions. Let's leave this locker room of preparation and venture onto the playing fields where victory awaits to the doers of what has been shared.

*****

If those words don't inspire and move you to greater production, I don't know what will. All of the "how to" books combined fall short in producing a schematic for success in comparison to this presentation. We no longer do have an excuse for mediocrity, for we have heard the call of greatness. Let's pursue it by applying what we learned here today. Thank you, Mr./Ms. speaker!

*****

I sincerely hope that each of us will apply the principles we heard today. Do not let your notes of this address remain merely in your mind or on scraps of paper, but let it be a blueprint for rising above the pack. Not only will that enhance your vocation, but it will show appreciation to our speaker.

*****

4-New Employee Welcomes

I welcome you to (name of company). I believe you have made a wise decision in joining our company. The work will not be easy, but nothing of value ever is easy. Your suggestions for making this a better company will always be valued. Again, welcome.

*****

Your presence here today denotes your desire to be a part of this valuable team. From the most tenured manager to the most recent employee, we welcome you to (company name).

*****

Welcome. As new members of the (company) team, you will play an important part in the operation and future of this company. We value you and hope you will jump right in and help to make this an even greater company. Let's go forward together.

*****

On behalf of the officials of (company name), I extend a heartfelt welcome to each of you. You are about to embark upon an adventure in commerce and we will do all we can to make it both meaningful and profitable. Welcome aboard!

*****

Welcome to our team. Each of you, over the next few months, will become an important part of this organization. You were chosen because of your potential, we expect that you will excel because of the energy you apply to the opportunity before you. To us, excellence is a daily way of life. Again, welcome.

*****

The entire staff of this company welcomes you to join us in our pursuit of business excellence. Your presence here testifies to your desire to be part of our goal. Thank you for your decision to join us and, again, welcome.

*****

Welcome. We will do everything we can to make you glad you decided to join us. The work will be hard yet rewarding, beneficial yet challenging, so join in, get involved and together we will continue to excel. Again, welcome!

*****

5-Welcome to Special Events (Picnics, Banquets, Etc.)

We are happy you could join us at the (name of event). May the events of this day foster friendship, fellowship and enable each of us to be better team members. Welcome and have a good time!

*****

It is always a pleasure to get together for events such as this. After countless hours of handwork, opportunities to unwind are greatly appreciated. So, I take special pleasure in welcoming each of you and your special guests to (name of event).

*****

One of the marks of asuccessful person is his/her ability to work hard and smart and play the same way. The human body can take just so much of each. There is no doubt that we have worked hard and smart. Today, we take great pleasure in welcoming you to (name of event) to play, and hope you will enjoy these hours of fellowship and fun.

*****

On behalf of (company name) I welcome you to this special event. There is no substitute for hard work...nor is there a substitute for good wholesome fellowship and fun. We are very proud of each of you and hope you will enjoy our time together today. Again, welcome!

*****

To each of you, we extend a hearty welcome! Each employee is a valued member of our great (company name) team. Please enjoy this time of social interaction and fun. Again, we welcome you.

*****

In our day-to-day duties, we seldom get to know each other on a personal basis. These types of events are designed to help us do that. You each represent a family that is as vital a part of this company as you are. We encourage you to not only talk with those you already know but to get to know people from other departments. On behalf of management, we heartily welcome each of you to (name of event).

*****

6-Farewell to Departing Employees

Many here today will be moving to other positions within our company while others will be leaving our company. We want to express our appreciation for your hard work. For those of you leaving, we thank you also and bid you the best in your future pursuits.

*****

Many of you have built precious professional and personal relationships during your tenure here. Those relationships helped to make you successful and helped our company to prosper. Our best wishes go with you for continued success in your future.

*****

Moving from one job to another brings reflection on the past and anticipation of a bright yet challenging future. Questions such as "will I like the people?" and "can I do the job?" sometimes dance through your mind. Nothing can allay these fears as well as a word of encouragement. To that end, I say that if you apply yourself in your new position, as well as you have here, you will be very successful. Go with our thanks for a job well done and best wishes and hopes for a bright future.

*****

First of all, I want to express my appreciation for your great service to this company. Without you, we would not enjoy the success we now experience and we regret your choice of leaving our company. We do not like losing good people. However, we respect your decision and wish you well.

*****

The best way to get a new job is to do well on your last one and each of you have been very successful here. Losing you is not something we look forward to, yet you must do what you must do. May you meet the challenges of your new job with the same vigor that you met the challenges here. We wish you a happy life and look forward to seeing you in the marketplace.

*****

"Goodbye" is not always easy to say to such distinguished employee(s). Yet as we say it we wish you much success in your future efforts and endeavors.

*****

7-Award Presentations

A company is not just corporations and offices, but a team of people dedicated to the common purpose of winning in their arena. Today, we are gathered to recognize some of those team members.

[Name each person and their accomplishment]

Please join me in applauding these people of distinction.

*****

It is a very special pleasure to take time to recognize the people and the achievements of the following persons:

[Name each person and their achievement]

Please join me in showing them how much we appreciate them.

*****

The following people have done wonderful jobs in their respective fields and it is a pleasure to present these awards to them. We can be proud of their hard and smart work. Each of them has an extraordinary desire to do the best job possible, and I am humbled and encouraged by them and their work ethic.

Please give them a show of appreciation.

*****

Awards are just a small way of showing appreciation for a job very well done. The greater appreciation comes from our respect for and emulation of their achievements. Let's dedicate ourselves to such excellence and show our respect in a hearty applause for these special people.

[Name each person and their accomplishment]

*****

Today, we are honored to present awards to the following people:

[Name each person and their achievement]

Our respect and appreciation go to each recipient along with our applause for a great job by each person.

*****

8-Building/Facilities Dedication

We are very honored today to break ground on this new building/facility. Because of your hard work, we have earned the opportunity to better serve more people. This facility will give us a place to fulfill that mission.

[Dedicators can either cut a ribbon or scoop a shovel of dirt]

*****

When you do a good job, it is often rewarded with more opportunities. Today, the dedication of this building/facility is a testament to the rewards of our labors. Our appreciation goes to you the workers who made this new building/facility possible. May your labors bring even richer rewards as this new edifice becomes a business place for customers old and new.

[Dedicators can either cut a ribbon or scoop a shovel of dirt]

*****

The expansion of this business is a tribute to the great services and products offered by all of you. Without you, this occasion would not have occurred. Our thanks go to you for your wonderful contribution. You are an integral part of this event. To you we now dedicate this building/facility.

[Dedicators may either cut a ribbon or scoop a shovel of dirt]

*****

With the [cutting of this ribbon or scooping of a shovel full of dirt] we enter an expanded era of service to our customers. Each of you made this building/facility possible. Thank you for joining us today at this great occasion.

*****

Because you have done such a great job, we need to expand. This expansion will enable us to serve even more people and your continued diligent service is encouraged and appreciated. You are this business and we now dedicate it to you.

[Dedicators can either cut a ribbon or scoop a shovel of dirt]

*****

9-Administrative Assistant Appreciation

No company has ever become great without a great secretary. Today, we pause to thank (secretary's name) for such a wonderful tenure of diligent service. This company is great because of her contributions.

*****

After the executives have made the decisions, the plan must be put into a legible format and distributed to the rest of the company. The secretary/administrative assistant make that a reality. The true extent of this secretary's contributions will probably never be known. However, today we want to show our appreciation to (secretary's name) for stellar service.

*****

A good secretary is an integral part of a company. Their work is often unseen but greatly appreciated. We are here to honor (secretary's name) for a continued performance of faithfulness and excellence. Please join me in applauding our distinguished honoree.

*****

Each day, tons of paper are transferred from one place to another. With the advent of e-commerce, millions of bytes go from place to place. Standing behind most of such transfers is a well-trained secretary. His/Her value is worth more than words can express. Thank you (secretary's name) for a job well done.

*****

Business is a complex system of transactions. These transactions require accuracy, speed and diligence. Millions of dollars can be lost by a transaction that is minutes late. The person usually responsible for coordinating the transactions is often the office secretary. Today, we are here to honor our secretary (secretary's name) for always "making it happen" for this company.

*****

A good secretary is often the motivator and coordinator for a company or office staff. The little things done by a secretary mean a lot. We publicly recognize (secretary's name). She/He is truly a faithful employee.

*****

10-Employee Promotions

A job well-done is often rewarded by a promotion. Today, it gives me great pleasure to announce the promotion of (person(s) name) to (title of promotion). Their hard and smart work is exemplary. They have set a pace for us all to follow. Please join me in showing our appreciation for what they have done (applause).

*****

Promotions are given for past performance and future expectations. Each of today's recipients exemplifies both. We pause to recognize them for their productive past and to encourage them in future efforts.

Our specific promotions are as follows:

(Name each person and their past and future positions followed by applause)

*****

The reward of hard work is often hard work---on another level--known as a promotion. Today, we celebrate the ascension of the following workers from one level of service to another. (Read each person's name and their promotion) Let's do our best to help each of these persons to succeed in their new jobs. For by doing that, you shall hasten the moment that you are promoted.

*****

A promotion is not just a "golden opportunity," but an opportunity to continue great service. With it comes higher responsibility and I charge each of you to remember that as you move into your new positions. I also thank all of you gathered here who made these promotions possible. The following people are being promoted (name persons and old and new jobs). Please join me in recognizing them.

*****

11-Supervisor Appreciation

A boss is nothing more than a servant occupying a higher level of responsibility. He/She is often the first one in the office and the last one to leave. Many of his/her decisions are sometimes unpleasant but often necessary. We are here to show our appreciation for our leader. He/She has made working here a pleasure. Please join me in an appreciative applause for (boss' name).

*****

Today, we are gathered to show thanks for our leader. As a result of his/her leadership, our department has excelled in our industry. When our leader wins, we win. Please join me in showing appreciation for a real winner (name).

*****

12-Words of Encouragement

We are so honored with the great work all of you have done. You epitomize everything that is good, wholesome and productive. May great success continue to follow you in everything you do.

*****

Thanks for your smart and hard work for this company. We appreciate you and will do all we can to insure your continued success.

*****

The accolades given to this company are only as good as its people. You represent the best and the brightest in your daily work. Thank you for doing what you do so well.

*****

I am so honored with what you have done to make this a company of the highest order. Your commitment to excellence has enabled us to be the best in our field. Be encouraged as you perform your daily duties because you are definitely making a difference.

*****

13-Holiday Salutations

On this occasion, we are thankful for a good year. Each of you has been a productive member of our team. May you enjoy to benefits of your labor and prosper in the coming days.

*****

Each year, we pause to reflect and express our appreciation for each of you. You are a valued and much appreciated member of our company. Because of you, we have made much progress this year and hope to build on our efforts in the coming year. We encourage you to spend time with your loved-ones and prepare for something even greater in the coming days.

*****

Thank you so much for your wonderful service during this past year. Each of you is an integral part of this company. Without you we would have nothing for which to brag. We encourage you to take time to enjoy your family and loved-ones and come back refreshed and ready to continue our trek towards greatness.

*****

Someone once said, "success is done as a team." During this season, we thank you for being part of our business team. We wish you the best as you take time to reflect and be with your family members. May the coming year bring growth and prosperity to each of you.

*****

Words Spoken During the Passing of a Team Member

Our hearts hurt deeply at this time of great loss. (Team Member Name) was a valued member of our team and their loss leaves a deep hole in our company. Our thoughts go out to their family members and loved-ones. May they receive the grace to grieve and to move forward in the coming days.

*****

Everyone in this company is appreciated and the loss of anyone is a painful event. Today, we acknowledge the loss of (Team Member Name). We shall dearly miss them. Their service to this company contributed greatly to the success of our mission. We stand resolutely with the family as they grieve in the coming days.

*****

As we grieve over the loss of (Team Member Name), we also pause to reflect upon their contribution to our company. (Team Member Name) served selflessly and helped us to accomplish great feats in our field. Today as we pause to remember them, we also pause to walk with their family as they grieve over their loss. Let us keep them in our thoughts in the days to come.

*****

We all grieve at the loss of (Team Member Name). (Team Member Name) served this company honorably for (Time Period). Their loss leaves a giant hole in the tapestry of our company. In the days to come, let each of us keep the family in our thoughts as they process the grief of this unexpected tragedy.

*****

14-Words of Appreciation

Today we are gathered here to express appreciation to (Name) for great service to our company. He/She has been an outstanding team player and great contributor to our mission success. (Name) we thank you for being there for all of us!

*****

Today we pause to thank someone very special in our organization. (Name) has worked faithfully as (various positions) for (time period). In that time he/she has been a team player and a team leader of the highest magnitude. Because of his/her service, we publicly thank him/her for outstanding service.

*****

Today we express appreciation for a job well-done. (Name) has helped our company to become a business leader. Let's congratulate (Name) for a great job.

*****

■■■

Join with me now as we show our appreciation for (Name). His/Her accomplishments include (list some). Because of his/her outstanding work, our company is positioned to make an impact in our industry. Let's hear it for (Name).

*****

Today, we pause to show public appreciation to someone who has labored diligently often in virtual obscurity. His/Her accomplishments include (list). We are fortunate to have someone of his/her abilities. Let's show our appreciation to (Name).

*****

We want to thank (Name) for outstanding service as (job position). His/Her dedication, commitment and diligence has been instrumental in making our company a leader in our industry. Let us give him/her a hand of gratitude!

www.ingramcontent.com/pod-product-compliance
Lightning Source LLC
Chambersburg PA
CBHW070136210526
45170CB00013B/1298